The Hay Ride

by Julia Zinal
illustrated by Peggy Tagel

HOUGHTON MIFFLIN BOSTON

Printed in China

ISBN-13: 978-0 547-01822-5
ISBN-10: 0-547-01822-3

8 9 10 0940 16 15 14 13
4500408731

See the hay.

See the wagon.

See the tractor.

See the farmer.

See the hay ride.

Responding

TARGET SKILL Text and Graphic Features Pick two pictures. Tell how the words go with the pictures.

Talk About It

Text to World Draw a picture. Show you and your family on a hay ride. Label your picture. Then tell about it.

to

TARGET SKILL **Text and Graphic Features** Tell how words go with art.

TARGET STRATEGY **Question** Ask questions about what you are reading.

GENRE **Informational text** gives facts about a topic.